Social Media

 Connect with a community of *Bible Studies for Life* users. Post responses to questions, share teaching ideas, and link to great blog content: facebook.com/biblestudiesforlife.

 Get instant updates about new articles, giveaways, and more: @BibleMeetsLife.

The App

Simple and straightforward, this elegantly designed iPhone app gives you all the content of the Bible study book—plus a whole lot more—right at your fingertips. Available in the iTunes App Store; search "Bible Studies for Life."

Blog

At biblestudiesforlife.com/blog you will find all the magazine articles we mention in this study guide and music downloads provided by LifeWay Worship. In addition, leaders and group members alike will benefit from the blog posts written for people in every life stage— singles, parents, boomers, and senior adults—as well as media clips, connections between our study topics, current events, and much more.

Training

 For helps on how to use Bible Studies for Life, tips on how to better lead groups, or additional ideas for leading this study, visit ministrygrid.com/web/biblestudiesforlife.

ISBN 978-1-4300-3498-8 • Item 00000000

Dewey decimal classification: 155.9
Subject headings: LIFE \ ENDURANCE \ JOSEPH, SON OF JACOB

Gena Rogers
Sam O'Neal
Content Editors

Brian Daniel
Manager, Short-Term Discipleship

Michael Kelley
Director, Discipleship and Groups Ministry

Send questions/comments to: Content Editor; *Bible Studies for Life: Adults;* One LifeWay Plaza; Nashville, TN 37234; or make comments on the web at biblestudiesforlife.com.

Printed in the United States of America

To order additional copies of this resource, write LifeWay Church Resources Customer Service; One LifeWay Plaza; Nashville, TN 37234; Fax order to 615.251.5933; call toll-free 800.458.2772; email orderentry@lifeway.com; or order online at www.lifeway.com.

Don't settle for survival. *You can overcome.*

Circumstances.

We all have them. Sometimes they're good. Sometimes they're bad. For so many people, the circumstances of life feel overwhelming. They can't change them, so they just learn to survive under them.

They simply endure.

Thankfully, that's not the life Christ calls us to live. He doesn't always remove our hardships, but He works through them and equips us to rise up and soar above them. Jesus overcame so that we can be overcomers.

The story of Joseph is more than a great tale filled with conflict and drama. By looking closely at Joseph's life, you will find motivation and practical help to live as an overcomer. Regardless of what's happening in your own life, you can be certain that God is at work for His good purpose.

So don't despair if life's circumstances are weighing heavily on you. Don't give up.

Just as surely as God had plans for Joseph, He also has plans for you!

Alex Himaya

Alex Himaya is the founding and senior pastor of theChurch, located in Tulsa, Oklahoma. theChurch is one of the fastest-growing churches in America. In its first 10 years of existence, it grew from 120 to 6,000 in attendance. theChurch has two campuses: theChurch at BattleCreek and theChurch at Midtown. Alex is also the founder of an international orphan-care ministry called Adopt(ed) and the author of *Jesus Hates Religion: Finding Grace in a Works-Driven Culture*. Alex and his wife, Meredith, have four children.

contents

SESSION 1

OVERCOME BETRAYAL

**What did sibling rivalry
look like at your house?**

QUESTION #1

#BSFLbetrayal

God is at work, even when it's not obvious.

THE BIBLE MEETS LIFE

Have you ever questioned the presence of God? I have.

My youngest son nearly drowned when he was two years old. In that terrifying moment—when all we knew was how close he was to death—it was hard to see God's hand anywhere. But despite everything we couldn't see, we chose to trust. Later, we saw clearly how God had been at work in so many details, right down to the ER nurse having the exact type of pacifier our boy loved. Our son survived, and we came away knowing God had been at work even before we cried out to Him.

We often think of God in moments of betrayal—whether we're betrayed by loved ones, trusted friends, or just by circumstances. We may even feel betrayed by God. Thankfully, God never betrays us. He's always working for our good, even when we don't realize it.

As we'll see in the Book of Genesis, Joseph was deeply affected when his own brothers betrayed him. Yet God was there the whole time, working on his behalf to help him move beyond betrayal.

WHAT DOES THE BIBLE SAY?

Genesis 37:19-27; 39:1-2 *(HCSB)*

37:19 They said to one another, "Here comes that dreamer!

20 Come on, let's kill him and throw him into one of the pits. We can say that a vicious animal ate him. Then we'll see what becomes of his dreams!"

21 When Reuben heard this, he tried to save him from them. He said, "Let's not take his life."

22 Reuben also said to them, "Don't shed blood. Throw him into this pit in the wilderness, but don't lay a hand on him"—intending to rescue him from their hands and return him to his father.

23 When Joseph came to his brothers, they stripped off his robe, the robe of many colors that he had on.

24 Then they took him and threw him into the pit. The pit was empty; there was no water in it.

25 Then they sat down to eat a meal. They looked up, and there was a caravan of Ishmaelites coming from Gilead. Their camels were carrying aromatic gum, balsam, and resin, going down to Egypt.

26 Then Judah said to his brothers, "What do we gain if we kill our brother and cover up his blood?

27 Come, let's sell him to the Ishmaelites and not lay a hand on him, for he is our brother, our own flesh," and they agreed.

....

39:1 Now Joseph had been taken to Egypt. An Egyptian named Potiphar, an officer of Pharaoh and the captain of the guard, bought him from the Ishmaelites who had brought him there.

2 The LORD was with Joseph, and he became a successful man, serving in the household of his Egyptian master.

Key Words

Pits (37:20)—These were deep holes dug as reservoirs for water collection and storage.

Robe (37:23)—A special garment of many colors or ornateness Jacob gave Joseph to signify Joseph as his favorite son (v. 3).

Genesis 37:19-24

It's hard to imagine a group of brothers wanting to kill one of their own, but that's what happened between Jacob's sons. We can't justify their aggression, but their jealousy had deep roots. For example, Jacob's wives were sisters with an intense rivalry, and his 12 sons came from four different mothers (see Gen. 29:30–30:4; 35:23-26). Worse, Jacob played favorites. He loved Joseph more than his other sons (see Gen. 37:4), and he gave Joseph a special robe (v. 3) that identified him as a prince or a person of distinction.

Joseph didn't help the situation. He tattled on his brothers (see v. 2), and he blabbed about two dreams that made him appear more important than the rest of his family—even his father and mother. For these reasons and more, Joseph found himself on the receiving end of his brothers' pent-up hatred. They were his family, but they turned on him like a pride of hungry lions. He was betrayed.

Too many of us learn the sting of betrayal at an early age. And sadly, we often relearn it in every season of life.

▶ You shared a secret with your best friend about a crush you had on someone, only to learn that your friend blabbed it to everyone in the class.

▶ Everyone was talking about an awesome party they went to on Saturday night, and you realized you were the only one not invited.

▶ Your parents said, "I do forever," but forever meant only until now.

▶ Someone took credit for your idea in the office and got the promotion you deserved.

Jesus knows what betrayal is like. Judas betrayed Him to the religious leaders, Peter publicly denied even knowing Him, and almost all the other disciples fled the scene when He was arrested.

> *What's your gut reaction to Joseph's betrayal?*

QUESTION #2

Worst of all, Jesus felt abandoned by His Father as He died on the cross. He cried out, "My God, My God, why have You forsaken me?" (Matt. 27:46).

The good news is that even in the midst of betrayal, you can trust that God has not abandoned you. You can rest assured that He is always involved in your life. Even when it's not obvious, He is at work!

> **What are our options when we feel betrayed?**
>
> QUESTION #3

STORIES OF BETRAYAL

Use the following chart to record one or two stories that feature a major act of betrayal. An example is provided to get you started.

Story Title	Act of Betrayal	Resolution
The Lion, the Witch, and the Wardrobe	Edmund betrays his siblings by helping the White Witch.	Edmund realizes his mistake and sides with Aslan.

What are some ways betrayals are typically resolved in real life?

Genesis 37:25-27

In one moment, Joseph went from meeting his brothers to staring death in the face. Being thrown in a pit must have hurt, but I'll bet his brothers' apathy hurt even more. As the brothers said years later, "We saw his deep distress when he pleaded with us, but we would not listen" (Gen. 42:21).

Then the brothers thought of a new plan: they could get rid of Joseph *and* make a quick buck at the same time! This idea presented itself when they saw a caravan of Ishmaelite traders headed their way. It was perfect—no fuss, no mess, and a little cash on the side.

God probably seemed completely absent to Joseph in that moment—but was He? Joseph was facing death, when a caravan suddenly came down the road. Some would write that off as coincidence; not me. The traders showed up at just the right time. Why? Because God wanted Joseph in Egypt. God was working behind the scenes to make sure he got there.

Let me state this again: God is always at work in your life—even when it's not obvious. Hold on to that truth when you feel you've been thrown into the pit. In addition, trusting that God is always at work will help you live with hope when you're tempted to feel guilt and regret over past shortcomings and failures.

For example, have any of these thoughts ever crossed your mind?

▶ I wasn't the faithful parent I should have been.

▶ I wasted parts of my life in sinful living.

▶ I didn't speak up for Jesus like I should have.

God works in all things—even our failures—for the good of His people. God can even work in our lives in spite of these things. He can take a trial and turn it into a testimony.

> **Since God is always at work, what's our responsibility when we can't see what He's doing?**

QUESTION **#4**

> "A false witness will not go unpunished,
> and one who utters lies will not escape."
>
> —PROVERBS 19:5

> Even after betrayal, how do we behave
> in ways that show God is at work?
>
> QUESTION #5

Genesis 39:1-2

Verse 2 sums up the main idea of this session: "The LORD was with Joseph." People may betray and abandon us, but God does not. No matter what it looks like from our perspective, God has not and will not abandon us. Joseph still may have questioned why all these things were happening to him, but he remained faithful to God—and God remained faithful to Him. God doesn't necessarily rescue us from all our difficulties, but we can be assured that He walks with us through them.

Only much later did Joseph see why God had allowed him to experience these events. It was God's plan all along for Joseph to have a powerful position in Egypt—a position that would ultimately keep his family alive during the famine and maintain the bloodline of the Messiah. Therefore, God's plan was accomplished even in the midst of something as destructive as betrayal.

Several years ago, I felt completely betrayed by one of my friends. We had been close, but suddenly something changed. He and I were on opposite sides of an invisible wall. We still are. On multiple occasions I've asked him to join me for coffee or a meal, hoping for a conversation—but each invitation is met with coldness and disinterest. At this stage I still feel betrayed and wronged, so what do I do? **I continue to trust that God will work all things together for my good.**

Joseph's example helps me trust God. Like Joseph, I may not see the different ways God is working in spite of the hurt and betrayal I feel. But I can still *know* that He is working. And I can still trust Him.

LIVE IT OUT

We choose our responses to betrayal. Here are some suggestions for trusting God even when you don't know what He's doing:

▶ **Look back.** Make a list of the different ways God has worked in and through your life in recent years.

▶ **Forgive yourself.** Identify a failure or shortcoming from the past that still produces guilt in your life. Choose to let go of that failure and trust in God's ability to work for your good.

▶ **Forgive others.** Identify a betrayal that continues to impact your life. Take a step this week to move toward forgiveness and healing in that relationship.

I'm sorry to say that you will experience betrayal. You will experience times when you cry out to God—maybe even times when you wonder if He's really there. Thankfully, God is at work even now to carry you through those moments, just as He carried Joseph.

Finding Your Way Out of the Desert

One of my favorite television shows is **Man vs. Wild,** *an ingenious reality show that attempts to show you how to survive in any number of hostile environments—from the Costa Rican rainforest to the Alaskan frontier to a wide array of desert locations. The host is an aptly named British gentleman named Bear Grylls, who parachutes into these remote locations, and spends a great deal of time running from, yes, bears, lions, and elephants.*

To continue reading "Finding Your Way Out of the Desert," visit biblestudiesforlife.com/articles.

My group's prayer requests

....
....
....
....
....
....
....
....
....
....
....
....

My thoughts

SESSION 2

OVERCOME TEMPTATION

What are some warning labels you always ignore?

#BSFLtemptation

It's easier to resist temptation when you know what's at stake.

THE BIBLE MEETS LIFE

It seems like everything comes with a warning label these days. These are often helpful, of course. But some warning labels are downright hilarious—including the following:

▶ On a hairdryer: "Do not use while sleeping."

▶ On a carton of eggs: "This product may contain eggs."

▶ On a scooter: "This product moves when used."

▶ On a small tractor: "Avoid death."[1]

We can laugh, but we also know there are times when we need to be warned. For example, wouldn't life be easier if temptations came with warning labels? Sin promises great things up front, but it's only after we give in that we learn about the consequences.

Joseph was a man who clearly saw the harmful consequences of giving in to temptation. His example can help us heed the warning labels we encounter as we face temptation each day.

WHAT DOES THE BIBLE SAY?

Genesis 39:3-12 *(HCSB)*

3 When his master saw that the LORD was with him and that the LORD made everything he did successful,

4 Joseph found favor in his master's sight and became his personal attendant. Potiphar also put him in charge of his household and placed all that he owned under his authority.

5 From the time that he put him in charge of his household and of all that he owned, the LORD blessed the Egyptian's house because of Joseph. The LORD's blessing was on all that he owned, in his house and in his fields.

6 He left all that he owned under Joseph's authority; he did not concern himself with anything except the food he ate. Now Joseph was well-built and handsome.

7 After some time his master's wife looked longingly at Joseph and said, "Sleep with me."

8 But he refused. "Look," he said to his master's wife, "with me here my master does not concern himself with anything in his house, and he has put all that he owns under my authority.

9 No one in this house is greater than I am. He has withheld nothing from me except you, because you are his wife. So how could I do such a great evil and sin against God?"

10 Although she spoke to Joseph day after day, he refused to go to bed with her.

11 Now one day he went into the house to do his work, and none of the household servants were there.

12 She grabbed him by his garment and said, "Sleep with me!" But leaving his garment in her hand, he escaped and ran outside.

Key Words

Blessed (v. 5)—In the Old Testament "bless" means "imbue with power for success and prosperity." God's blessings fulfilled His promise to bless those who blessed Abraham (Gen. 12:3).

Garment (v. 12)—Could refer to either outer or inner clothing. Some argue Joseph left the inner garment, but we should not think Joseph ran from the house naked.

Genesis 39:3-6

Joseph wasn't where he wanted to be. Betrayed by his brothers, he was no longer seen as the favored son of a wealthy man. Instead, he was a slave. In Egypt, Joseph became the property of a man named Potiphar. We know little about this man, except what we're told in Genesis 39. The key thing to remember is that Potiphar saw the hand of God on Joseph:

▶ Joseph's master "saw that the LORD was with him" (v. 3).

▶ "The LORD made everything he did successful" (v. 3).

▶ "The LORD blessed the Egyptian's house because of Joseph" (v. 5).

▶ "The LORD's blessing was on all that he owned, in his house and in his fields" (v. 5).

God was with Joseph, even though His presence wasn't always clear. It's true that God eventually brought Joseph full circle and blessed him in tangible ways. But even in the darkest moments, God was there.

What I find interesting is the way God's presence in Joseph's life became a blessing to others:

▶ Potiphar became wealthy and prospered (39:5).

▶ Pharaoh's kingdom was rescued from the famine (see Gen. 41).

▶ Joseph's family was preserved through the famine (see Gen. 42–43).

God doesn't bless us so that we can hoard His blessings. Rather, He blesses us so that we can serve as a blessing to those around us. In other words, with blessing comes responsibility.

What characteristics suggest God is with someone?

QUESTION **#2**

Joseph served with great faithfulness. Verse 6 sums up Joseph's integrity: Potiphar "did not concern himself with anything except the food he ate." The Hebrew phrase translated "did not concern himself" literally says Potiphar "did not know what was in his house." Joseph took care of things to such a degree that Potiphar didn't have to think about them at all!

WHAT'S AT STAKE?

TECHNOLOGY   **MONEY**   **ENTERTAINMENT**

Choose one of the above tools. How has that tool benefitted our culture in recent years?

What's at stake for our culture when these tools become twisted into sources of temptation?

Genesis 39:7-10

Potiphar not only trusted Joseph with his house and his fields, but also with his wife. He believed Joseph was trustworthy. At the same time, Joseph knew his behavior needed to reflect that trust in order to remain esteemed by his master.

Sadly, because of Potiphar's wife, Joseph had to continually stand his ground in order to remain faithful. Day in and day out, she attempted to seduce Joseph. She tempted him to do wrong.

But Joseph stood firm in the face of temptation. Time after time, "he refused to go to bed with her" (39:10).

Notice that Joseph put a roadblock at the top of the mountain instead of a first aid station at the bottom. Instead of setting a plan in place to fix a problem, he set a plan in place to make sure there wasn't a problem to begin with.

Why? Because Joseph knew what was at stake.

In the early days of Billy Graham's ministry, he met with his evangelistic team to discuss the pitfalls and criticisms that had damaged the credibility of several evangelists. That meeting produced the "Modesto Manifesto." One of the standards they set in place was to avoid any appearance of sexual impropriety. Billy Graham made it a point to never travel, meet, or eat alone with any woman other than his own wife, Ruth.

Joseph obviously had similar convictions. We know from verse 9 that he valued his position in Potiphar's house—and valued even more his relationship with God. Again, he knew what was at stake.

Potiphar's wife didn't make her move once and give up. She persisted. And Joseph persisted in saying no. In fact, Joseph's perseverance may have been challenged for as long as 11 years! I doubt Joseph could have held firm without a relationship with God—and the conviction to maintain that relationship no matter what.

> **What's at stake when we give in to temptation?**
>
> QUESTION **#3**

> **What's at stake when we resist temptation?**
>
> QUESTION **#4**

Genesis 39:11-12

We should avoid temptation whenever possible. But there will still be times when temptation is unavoidable and demands a response. That's what happened to Joseph.

When you think about it, verse 11 describes an ideal opportunity for Joseph to give up his principles and give in to temptation. The house was empty. Potiphar's wife literally threw herself at him in her zeal for an affair. No one else was around, which meant no one would know about any wrongdoing—that is, no one except Joseph, Potiphar's wife, and God.

Once again, Joseph didn't hesitate in making the right choice. He fled the scene in order to retain his integrity. It's important for us to remember that even when we're as careful as we can be to avoid temptation, we may still find ourselves in situations where the only option is to do what Joseph did: run!

Unfortunately, Potiphar's wife chose to lie about what happened. With Joseph's abandoned cloak as evidence, she accused him of attacking her. Despite his righteous actions, Joseph ended up in prison (see vv. 13-20). Someone might ask, "What's the benefit of resisting temptation if it still lands you in hot water?" We'll find the answer to that question as we continue exploring Joseph's story in the weeks to come. Yes, Joseph paid a price for his moral stand, but it wasn't final. In the end, God was at work even in Joseph's darkest days and ultimately brought him to a place of prominence, influence, and full restoration with his family.

> **What's the difference between resisting temptation and fleeing from temptation?**

QUESTION **#5**

LIVE IT OUT

We all encounter temptation from time to time. Consider the following suggestions for making the right choice:

▶ **Look inside.** The first step in fleeing temptation is recognizing that temptation springs from our own desires (see Jas. 1:14). Spend a few moments evaluating which inner desires often tempt you to do wrong.

▶ **Remember what's at stake.** When faced with temptation, we always have a choice. Choose to consider the consequences (spiritual, relational, physical, etc.) *before* you choose to sin.

▶ **Remember God's Word.** Memorize 1 Corinthians 10:13 as a reminder that temptation always creates a choice.

So much in our culture is designed to pull us away from God's plan and God's commands. But read the warning label whenever you face temptation. There's always more at stake than meets the eye.

Idols Away

Picture an eight-year-old boy's messy room. It's scattered with action figures, books, and games. Don't forget to watch your step for Legos® lying low like land mines. And then there's that little boy who's been playing outside. His stench fills the room too. Whew! Now imagine the ancient nation of Judah in a bigger mess. There were no Legos® in Judah. It was much worse—idols, false worship, and heinous activities had overtaken the nation. Judah needed spring cleaning as it had never known.

To continue reading "Idols Away" from *HomeLife* magazine, visit biblestudiesforlife.com/articles.

My group's prayer requests

....

....

....

....

....

....

....

....

....

....

....

....

....

My thoughts

1. Brett Nelson and Katy Finneran, "Dumbest Warning Labels," www.forbes.com, published February 23, 2011, accessed March 17, 2014.

SESSION 3

OVERCOME BEING FORGOTTEN

When have you rediscovered something you forgot you had?

#BSFLforgotten

QUESTION #1

Keep doing what God has gifted you to do.

THE BIBLE MEETS LIFE

When my oldest child was around five years old, I forgot her and left her at a restaurant several states away from home.

We were on vacation in Florida, traveling in a large SUV with three rows of seats. As our family left the restaurant, my daughter slipped into a game room near the exit. She always sat in the back of the car and kept to herself, content within a nest of books and blankets. So, my wife and I assumed she had already hopped in as we buckled the other kids into their car seats. It wasn't until we pulled into the driveway of our rental home five miles away that my wife asked, "Where's Katherine?"

Have you ever felt forgotten? Ever felt like the world has passed you by—like friends and family have gone on to bigger and better things and you're just stuck? Ever felt like even God has forgotten you?

The life of Joseph offers proof that God doesn't forget you. He's always aware of your circumstances. And, like Joseph, you can choose positive action while you wait to see what God is doing in your life.

WHAT DOES THE BIBLE SAY?

Genesis 39:21-23; 40:5-8,20-23 *(HCSB)*

39:21 But the LORD was with Joseph and extended kindness to him. He granted him favor in the eyes of the prison warden.

22 The warden put all the prisoners who were in the prison under Joseph's authority, and he was responsible for everything that was done there.

23 The warden did not bother with anything under Joseph's authority, because the LORD was with him, and the LORD made everything that he did successful.

40:5 The Egyptian king's cupbearer and baker, who were confined in the prison, each had a dream. Both had a dream on the same night, and each dream had its own meaning.

6 When Joseph came to them in the morning, he saw that they looked distraught.

7 So he asked Pharaoh's officers who were in custody with him in his master's house, "Why do you look so sad today?"

8 "We had dreams," they said to him, "but there is no one to interpret them." Then Joseph said to them, "Don't interpretations belong to God? Tell me your dreams."

40:20 On the third day, which was Pharaoh's birthday, he gave a feast for all his servants. He lifted up the heads of the chief cupbearer and the chief baker.

21 Pharaoh restored the chief cupbearer to his position as cupbearer, and he placed the cup in Pharaoh's hand.

22 But Pharaoh hanged the chief baker, just as Joseph had explained to them.

23 Yet the chief cupbearer did not remember Joseph; he forgot him.

Key Words

Cupbearer (40:5)—A staff supervisor and responsible for tasting the ruler's wine before serving it to him to ensure it did not contain poison. Often the cupbearer became the ruler's confidant and adviser.

Lifted up the heads (40:20)—The phrase "lifted up the heads" carried a double meaning: restoration for the cupbearer and death for the chief baker.

Genesis 39:21-23

It's clear once again that God was with Joseph at every turn—even when it may have appeared otherwise. Not only that, but Joseph remained faithful to God by continuing to do what God had gifted him to do. God had equipped Joseph to dream and to lead; therefore, Joseph exercised those gifts by managing with excellence even in the depths of an Egyptian prison.

We also need to be aware of what God has gifted us to do. In His sovereignty, God knit you together in your mother's womb (see Ps. 139:13). He made you to fit into His body, the church, just the way He wants you to fit (see 1 Cor. 12:12-31). So we, like Joseph, must take our individual gifting and abilities seriously. **Even when we face difficulty, we can—and we certainly should—continue to use the gifts God has given us.**

Look at Joseph's situation. He went from being the favored son of Jacob to being a slave, but he served with excellence. Now he had gone from being a slave to a prisoner. His position went from bad to worse. We don't know what Joseph did to distinguish himself in prison, but he did it with excellence. Consequently, he was given responsibility and authority. An Egyptian prison surely was a far cry from where Joseph expected to be, but instead of wallowing in self-pity, he continued to serve.

I don't love God by attempting to do something I have no business doing. For example, He has not designed me to lead others in praise and worship. I can't sing at all and am not musical in the least. (That's what I've been told. By everyone.) So, I can rest assured knowing that's not what God created me to do. But God has equipped me to serve as a pastor. Therefore, when I express love to Him and others by preaching, I'm doing what God gifted me to do. Consequently, I know that I'm following His will.

> *How do we remain faithful when we find ourselves where we didn't expect to be?*
>
> QUESTION #2

Genesis 40:5-8

One day a couple of new prisoners were added to the prison population: Pharaoh's cupbearer and chief baker. We don't know what their specific crimes were, but they had obviously offended Pharaoh and made him angry enough to toss them into prison.

Having proven himself responsible, Joseph was assigned to be the personal attendant to both the cupbearer and baker (see Gen. 40:4). This assignment implies that these were men of rank. More than just men in charge of the wine cellar and bakery, they were also advisers to Pharaoh. Verse 7 refers to them as "Pharaoh's officers." They may have been prisoners at that moment, but it became Joseph's duty to wait on them.

Joseph did more than his duty to merely serve these men. He showed genuine concern for them when they became distraught. Noticing their sadness, Joseph asked how he could help. Such compassion surely was beyond his job description.

That same night both men had troubling dreams—dreams they could not understand and no one could interpret. Joseph agreed to help and told them the ability to interpret dreams came from God. No doubt, God gave him great insight (v. 8), and Joseph's skill in interpreting dreams was another indication that God was still with him. Joseph pointed to God, and it certainly appeared that God was working His will in Joseph's life through the dreams.

Joseph was 17 when he went to Egypt (see Gen. 37:2) and 30 when he was delivered from prison (see Gen. 41:46). He spent 13 years as a servant and a prisoner. Joseph eventually became the second in command over Egypt, but he first experienced 13 years of discipline, training, and preparation. His path to a position of great authority and leadership was a path of humble service to others.

What are some little things that allow us to demonstrate God's concern to others?

QUESTION #3

Genesis 40:20-23

Joseph showed compassion in helping the baker and cupbearer, and he faithfully shared what God had revealed to him regarding their dreams. Joseph made only one request in return: "But when all goes well for you, remember that I was with you. Please show kindness to me by mentioning me to Pharaoh, and get me out of this prison" (see Gen. 40:14).

> **When have you felt forgotten?**
>
> QUESTION #4

What came of that request? "Yet the chief cupbearer did not remember Joseph; he forgot him" (v. 23). Joseph was forgotten. Worse, he was forgotten by someone he had helped!

Let me return to the time I forgot my daughter. I must have driven 100 mph back to the restaurant. When I pulled up, a bus load of senior adults had gathered on the front porch. Apparently they had been standing there when I drove off—they'd watched Katherine run behind my car screaming, "Daddy! Daddy! Daddy!" They were *not* happy with me.

Kind folks at the restaurant had taken my daughter to the kitchen while they waited, hoping for her parents to return. Katherine had given them my cell phone number, of course, but my daughter wasn't the only thing I forgot in that restaurant. I also left my phone on the table. (It was a long trip.) So, when they tried to call me, my phone began to ring in a waitress's apron.

Here's the point: it's true that I unintentionally left my daughter in a strange place, but that didn't mean I loved her any less. I didn't forget her because she wasn't valuable to me. It was just a mistake.

Thankfully, God never forgets us. Unlike imperfect humans, He never makes mistakes. Therefore, we can remain confident in His plan even when it seems like we've been left out of that plan. We may *feel* like God is absent, but we can *know* He is still there, always loving us and watching over us.

Joseph surely felt forgotten, but he didn't quit. Tragedy is not terminal. Disappointment is not the final chapter. Pain is not the ultimate end for a child of God. He gets the final word. Always! When we allow this truth to be hidden in our hearts, quitting isn't an option—even when we feel forgotten.

> *How do we support one another to keep doing what God has gifted us to do?*

QUESTION #5

YOUR GIFT

What's one of the primary ways God has gifted you to do His work?

Record ideas for using that gift in the following spheres of life.

Church	Family	Community	Work

LIVE IT OUT

You have options for remaining engaged even when you feel forgotten in life. Consider the following:

▶ **Discover your gifts.** Use a spiritual-gifts assessment to identify the ways God has equipped you to serve.

▶ **Sharpen your skills.** Use a tool like the Ministry Grid (*MinistryGrid.com*) to gain training for different areas of ministry that connect with your natural gifts.

▶ **Make a difference.** Jump in with both feet to serve God and others. Find an area of need in your church or community, and use your gifts to serve with excellence.

God loves you and values you deeply as His child. But that doesn't mean you'll avoid feeling forgotten at different moments in your life. The good news is that you can choose to make a positive impact during those moments, as Joseph did.

Four Simple Words

During the Korean War I was a gunner on a B-29 bomber. My most memorable experience occurred when two engines went out and we landed amid a brilliant ball of fire. It was an exciting day, but it was not the one that changed my life forever.

To continue reading "Four Simple Words" from *Mature Living* magazine, visit biblestudiesforlife.com/articles.

My group's prayer requests

....

....

....

....

....

....

....

....

....

....

....

My thoughts

SESSION 4

OVERCOME HARD TIMES

What is your number one survival tip to prepare for a crisis?

QUESTION **#1**

#BSFLhardtimes

God has a plan to see you through any crisis.

THE BIBLE MEETS LIFE

"The house is on fire!" That's the first thing my friend heard after receiving a phone call from his wife on an otherwise normal day.

Two hours later, firemen escorted my friend and his wife into what was left of their home. In that brief time, their lives had been unbelievably impacted, their needs became dramatic, and their foreseeable future was unsure.

Sometimes we can see a crisis looming in the distance. Yet other times we're caught totally off guard by something huge that changes our lives in a moment. Thankfully, that's not the case for God. No matter how shocked we may feel in moments of crisis, He's never surprised or unprepared.

The Book of Genesis records how God prepared and led Joseph to make provision for the people of Egypt during the hard times they were about to experience. The life of Joseph demonstrates that God does what He says He will do—and that even in the face of a problem, God has the answer we need.

WHAT DOES THE BIBLE SAY?

Genesis 41:28-36,46-49 *(HCSB)*

28 "It is just as I told Pharaoh: God has shown Pharaoh what He is about to do. 29 Seven years of great abundance are coming throughout the land of Egypt. 30 After them, seven years of famine will take place, and all the abundance in the land of Egypt will be forgotten. The famine will devastate the land. 31 The abundance in the land will not be remembered because of the famine that follows it, for the famine will be very severe. 32 Since the dream was given twice to Pharaoh, it means that the matter has been determined by God, and He will carry it out soon.

33 "So now, let Pharaoh look for a discerning and wise man and set him over the land of Egypt. 34 Let Pharaoh do this: Let him appoint overseers over the land and take a fifth of the harvest of the land of Egypt during the seven years of abundance. 35 Let them gather all the excess food during these good years that are coming. Under Pharaoh's authority, store the grain in the cities, so they may preserve it as food. 36 The food will be a reserve for the land during the seven years of famine that will take place in the land of Egypt. Then the country will not be wiped out by the famine."

46 Joseph was 30 years old when he entered the service of Pharaoh king of Egypt. Joseph left Pharaoh's presence and traveled throughout the land of Egypt. 47 During the seven years of abundance the land produced outstanding harvests. 48 Joseph gathered all the excess food in the land of Egypt during the seven years and put it in the cities. He put the food in every city from the fields around it. 49 So Joseph stored up grain in such abundance—like the sand of the sea—that he stopped measuring it because it was beyond measure.

Key Words

Discerning (v. 33)—The Hebrew word translated "discerning" means "to consider, perceive, distinguish" and indicates someone with true insight into things, as distinguished from "wise," which indicates sharp administrative skills.

Genesis 41:28-32

Remember Joseph's backstory? He was thrown in prison when Potiphar's wife wrongly accused him of attacking her. Even after interpreting the dreams of Pharaoh's chief baker and cupbearer, Joseph remained forgotten in prison for two years. It wasn't until two other dreams needed interpretation—dreams Pharaoh himself had—that the cupbearer remembered Joseph (see Gen. 41:1-14). In a moment, Joseph went from being a forgotten man in prison to standing before all the splendor of Pharaoh.

Notice that Joseph acknowledged God as the One who would supply the meaning of Pharaoh's dreams. He didn't attempt to grab the credit for himself. Pharaoh's two dreams involved seven healthy cows followed by seven weak, sickly cows; and seven healthy stalks of grain followed by seven withered, dry stalks. Under God's direction, Joseph showed that these dreams pointed to seven years of abundance followed by seven years of famine.

Joseph identified two challenges for Pharaoh. The first was how to make the best use of the time of prosperity on the horizon. The second was to find a way to avoid the destruction of Pharaoh's people. God would provide a time of great prosperity, which can also be translated "great satisfaction"—but it was to help them prepare for the dark and difficult times ahead. The time of famine would be so difficult that the emptiness and hunger of the people would replace the great satisfaction they had once enjoyed.

God always has a purpose to what He puts in our hands. Whether it's an abundant harvest of crops; success in the workplace; a bonus check; or additional skills, assets, or relationships; they each represent a way God is preparing us for what lies ahead.

> **What does God's warning tell us about His character?**
>
> QUESTION #2

Genesis 41:33-36

Joseph mapped out a survival plan for the next 14 years. He offered a strategy to prevent starvation and a plan to shield Egypt's prosperity from ruin. By setting aside 20 percent of the abundant harvest each year, empowering a capable leadership team, and building suitable storage facilities with appropriate safeguards, Joseph scripted a menu to feed the people for the seven lean years to come.

It was a solid plan.

Maybe God gave the plan to Joseph in that moment, and Joseph subsequently relayed God's message to Pharaoh and his court. Maybe the plan came out of knowledge God had poured into Joseph through his previous experiences growing up in a farming family, managing Potiphar's household, and administrating while in the prison. **Either way, the ultimate Source of the plan was God.**

In the midst of adversity, Joseph rose to the occasion, with God's help. When he was sold, he served faithfully. When he was betrayed, he bounced back. When he was humbled, he worked his way up. Joseph had learned how to match what he had with what needed to be accomplished. In this moment before Pharaoh, he put those God-given skills and experience to work.

We've all sat in classes or training where we've thought: "I am never going to need this." But God never gives us anything we don't need. If we keep our eyes open, He will provide us the opportunity to apply what we have experienced and learned.

Of course, the first part of Joseph's plan was to find an intelligent and wise person capable of carrying it out. Some interpretations say a "discerning" man—literally a man with understanding. The new guy, straight from the prison with a fresh bath and haircut, got right to the heart of the matter: "Pharaoh, if we are to survive this, we need a leader."

When has God given you a clear picture of what to do?

QUESTION **#3**

Genesis 41:46-49

Joseph, a prisoner, boldly gave the head of Egypt a plan of action. And Pharaoh wisely saw that Joseph was the very one to carry out that plan. Joseph was given complete authority over the nation of Egypt, second only to Pharaoh himself. He was given Pharaoh's own signet ring and a chain of gold, which can be interpreted from the Hebrew as a knitted collar of gold for his neck. Pharaoh also gave Joseph a wife with high social standing (see Gen. 41:37-45).

Joseph could have said, "Finally, the good life and a chance to sit back and relax." Instead, Joseph left the comfort of the palace and got to work. Verse 46 tells us "Joseph left Pharaoh's presence" and went to work. He wasted no time. He inspected the entire land of Egypt. He wanted to understand every resource he had at his disposal to accomplish the great task in front of him.

I have a friend who worked for years with Sam Walton, the founder of Wal-Mart. He told me Sam would often say, "Never lead from your chair." That describes Joseph. He was a doer who stayed focused and on track. All the hard work, planning, and storing weren't for the good times; they were for the future. This was their insurance in the face of the impending disaster to come.

Let me take you back to my friend whose house caught fire. Much of their house was burned, and what wasn't burned was damaged by smoke. They left on the night of the fire with nothing but the clothes they were wearing. If that were the end of the story, it would certainly be tragic. But it wasn't the end. My friend had purchased insurance. He had planned for the unknown—for potential crisis. And when that crisis hit, he was covered. The insurance company immediately went to work, and five months later, his family moved into a new house.

God directed Joseph to a wise plan for the nation, and Joseph worked that plan. As a result, Joseph was used by God to save a nation.

> *When we don't have a clear picture from God, how can we actively pursue His solution?*

QUESTION **#4**

> *How is God preparing our group for present and future challenges?*

QUESTION **#5**

"The best-laid schemes o' mice and men often go awry."

—ROBERT BURNS

YOUR PLAN

Use the road map below to record your potential plans and goals over the next 20 years.

1 Year	
5 Years	
20 Years	

What are some ways your plans can connect with God's continuing plan for the world?

LIVE IT OUT

Since we're best served by following God's plan during a crisis, what should we do in the meantime? Consider the following:

▶ **Look behind.** Make a list of the ways God has prepared you for where you are today. Be specific.

▶ **Look up.** Set aside time this week to thank God for His provision in your life. Praise Him as the Source of your successes and of your ability to handle trials.

▶ **Look around.** Make yourself available to others. Ask the Lord to lead you to someone this week who is in difficulty or crisis, and use your gifts to help in a practical way.

Lord willing, you'll never experience a house in flames. But you will go through hard times. You'll have to make decisions in the middle of a crisis. And in that moment, you'll do well to remember that God already has a plan to see you through.

This Too Shall Pass

Are you in a difficult situation? Is your patience being tried, giving new meaning to the word exasperation? If so, you are not alone. As the saying goes, there are three kinds of people in the world—those who are currently in trouble, those who have just come out of trouble, and those who are about to get into trouble.

To continue reading "This Too Shall Pass" from *Mature Living* magazine, visit biblestudiesforlife.com/articles.

My group's prayer requests

My thoughts

SESSION 5

OVERCOME BITTERNESS

How would you describe
the taste of bitterness?

#BSFLbitterness

Relationships can only move forward with forgiveness.

THE BIBLE MEETS LIFE

Let's admit it: forgiving another person can be hard. Really hard.

During a routine sweep of Central Park, NYPD officer Steven McDonald was shot in the back of the head three times by a 15-year-old kid. Because of that momentary act of violence, Steven has spent the last 28 years confined to a wheelchair as a quadriplegic. He hasn't held his wife in two decades. He has never held or played catch with his son, who was born just a few months after the shooting.

But Steven *has* forgiven the young man who shot him. "I forgave him because I believe the only thing worse than receiving a bullet in my spine would have been to nurture revenge in my heart," he said. "Such an attitude would have extended my injury to my soul, hurting my wife, son, and others even more. … I have come to realize that anger is a wasted emotion."[1]

In our study of Joseph's life, we've seen a man who had every reason to feel hurt, angry, and bitter. But he chose forgiveness, instead.

WHAT DOES THE BIBLE SAY?

Genesis 45:3-11 *(HCSB)*

3 Joseph said to his brothers, "I am Joseph! Is my father still living?" But they could not answer him because they were terrified in his presence.

4 Then Joseph said to his brothers, "Please, come near me," and they came near. "I am Joseph, your brother," he said, "the one you sold into Egypt.

5 And now don't be worried or angry with yourselves for selling me here, because God sent me ahead of you to preserve life.

6 For the famine has been in the land these two years, and there will be five more years without plowing or harvesting.

7 God sent me ahead of you to establish you as a remnant within the land and to keep you alive by a great deliverance.

8 Therefore it was not you who sent me here, but God. He has made me a father to Pharaoh, lord of his entire household, and ruler over all the land of Egypt.

9 "Return quickly to my father and say to him, 'This is what your son Joseph says: "God has made me lord of all Egypt. Come down to me without delay.

10 You can settle in the land of Goshen and be near me—you, your children, and grandchildren, your sheep, cattle, and all you have.

11 There I will sustain you, for there will be five more years of famine. Otherwise, you, your household, and everything you have will become destitute."'"

Genesis 45:3-4

While God's warning and Joseph's plan helped Egypt survive the famine, others didn't fare so well. Jacob and his family were among those who suffered, which meant they were forced to join the many nations coming to Egypt for grain. Genesis 42–44 tells about a series of tests Joseph put his brothers through when they arrived in Egypt—tests designed to reveal any changes in their character. It was only after Judah offered his own life in place of Benjamin's (see Gen. 44:18-34) that Joseph revealed who he was, welcoming his brothers back into his world.

Declaring "I am Joseph" must have been a powerful moment for Joseph, but what happened afterward certainly could have gone differently. Joseph could have followed his introduction by asking, "How do you like my coat now? Ever been in a pit? Let me introduce you to one." Such statements may have been justified based on the way his brothers had treated him years earlier. However, after revealing his identity, Joseph exposed his values and longing by asking, "Is my father still living?"

What a moment for Joseph's brothers! In an instant, the weight of their guilt and lies was exchanged for a heart-stopping realization that the next few moments might be their last. Joseph could have ended their lives simply by waving his hand. Instead, Joseph invited them to come closer.

The brothers received an invitation to be restored in their relationship. The dreamer they had once despised so severely and had removed from their presence offered them a chance to come close again. They were given a second chance: the burden of their lies removed, the relationship repaired, and forgiveness extended. Only Joseph had the power to make this happen.

> *How can we let go of the past without forgetting it?*

QUESTION **#2**

Genesis 45:5-8

Joseph added another amazing statement: it was all God's plan. Not only did Joseph's words imply forgiveness, they also allowed his brothers to see that they'd all been instruments in God's plan.

The brothers had paid a high price all their lives for the awful thing they'd done to Joseph. His caring words to them were "Don't be worried or angry with yourselves," which can also be translated, "Don't grieve."

Grief is such a powerful emotion. Its effects can include nausea, insomnia, and depression—all of which can last for years. The longer the grieving process, the greater the impact on the individual. Have you ever noticed someone's demeanor and immediately knew he or she must be carrying a heavy burden? Joseph saw that in his brothers and said, "Don't be worried or angry with yourselves."

Joseph gave his brothers permission to stand tall. He said it was God and not his brothers who had sent him there to Egypt.

▶ God brought a caravan at just the right time (see Gen. 37:25).

▶ God "introduced" Joseph to the baker and the cupbearer (see Gen. 40:2-4).

▶ God sent the dreams to Pharaoh and gave Joseph the ability and the opportunity to interpret his dreams and offer a plan of action (see Gen. 41:25-36).

God is at work in your life also, even in difficult and trying circumstances. Consider that God may be using difficult situations (and difficult people) to bring you into a better place and a closer walk with Him. Don't hold those circumstances against the other people involved. **Allow God to work through your heartfelt, honest words—words that could speak freedom and forgiveness.**

When have you been willing to forgive?

QUESTION **#3**

Genesis 45:9-11

Restoration is an amazing thing. In session four I mentioned my friend whose house had burned down. He later told me about moving back into their renovated home. He and his wife walked through the new front door onto the new ceramic tile that had replaced the old, dark-brown flooring. There were new cabinets and plumbing, new lights, new closets, and a new fireplace with a beautiful new mantel. He told me later he could hardly remember what the house looked like before the fire.

A restored home is nice, but a restored relationship is truly amazing.

When Joseph covered the relationship with his brothers in forgiveness, all of their lives gained a new color and a new texture. The doorway of resentment and hurt was pulled down and replaced with an entrance into love and mutual concern. They started walking on a new foundation in their relationship that no longer was cracked, broken, or worn out from betrayal and lies; they walked on hope instead. It was a new day indeed.

> *How did Joseph's actions in this story mirror God's actions toward us?*
>
> QUESTION **#4**

Joseph knew one man still was filled with mourning and sorrow: his father, Jacob. Joseph directed his brothers to leave immediately and to tell their father the news. They were to tell the truth this time. Jacob's 13-year time of grief finally would turn to joy; he surely would remember the dreams Joseph had spoken of as a teenager (see Gen. 37:5-11) and realize they had come to pass.

The separation between Joseph and his family involved much more than the desert sand and rocky mountains between them. Their relationships had been broken. But Joseph wished for intimacy again. And just like in verse 4 when he asked his brothers to come closer, in verse 10 he emphasized his desire for family closeness again. "Settle in the land of Goshen and be near me."

> *What actions on our part begin and maintain the process of reconciliation?*
>
> QUESTION **#5**

The space between them was removed with forgiveness.

"Forgiveness is an act of the will, and the will can function regardless of the temperature of the heart."

—CORRIE TEN BOOM

Listen to the song "Bend" by Brandon Heath as a way of reflecting on Joseph's larger story. (Using an app to read the QR Code below will link to the song on Worship-HouseMedia.com.)

Use the space provided to record your reactions to that story. Don't be afraid to get creative by expressing yourself through a picture, a list of emotions, your own song, etc.

LIVE IT OUT

How can you incorporate forgiveness into your everyday life? Consider the following steps:

▶ **Connect with family.** Take time this week to intentionally connect with a family member. Invest in your relationships as a preventative measure against bitterness and strife.

▶ **Identify your hurts.** Think through the major pain points that cause you to harbor unforgiveness against others. Ask God to help you understand those hurts, but also to forgive even as He has forgiven you.

▶ **Apologize when necessary.** If you've wronged someone, acknowledge it. Be bold in asking for forgiveness.

It's hard to let go of the hurt others have caused. Sometimes it seems nearly impossible. But it's worth the effort. Why? Because the taste of forgiveness is far sweeter than the taste of bitterness.

I'd Love You All Over Again

I was completely caught off guard. Thinking that we were going to have lunch with friends, I didn't question my wife, Melody, when she jumped into the driver's seat. It was our fifth anniversary, and I probably should've been aware that she was up to something. While she drove, I returned a phone call and didn't realize anything was out of the ordinary until she made a turn in the opposite direction of our friends' neighborhood. Rather than offer an explanation, she reached into the console and handed me an envelope.

To continue reading "I'd Love You All Over Again" from *HomeLife* magazine, visit biblestudiesforlife.com/articles.

My group's prayer requests

....
....
....
....
....
....
....
....
....
....
....

My thoughts

1. CBS New York, "25 Years Later, Paralyzed NYPD Detective McDonald Still Inspiring Others," http://newyork.cbslocal.com/2011/07/12/25, July 12, 2011, accessed March 3, 2014.

SESSION 6

OVERCOME AN EARTHLY MINDSET

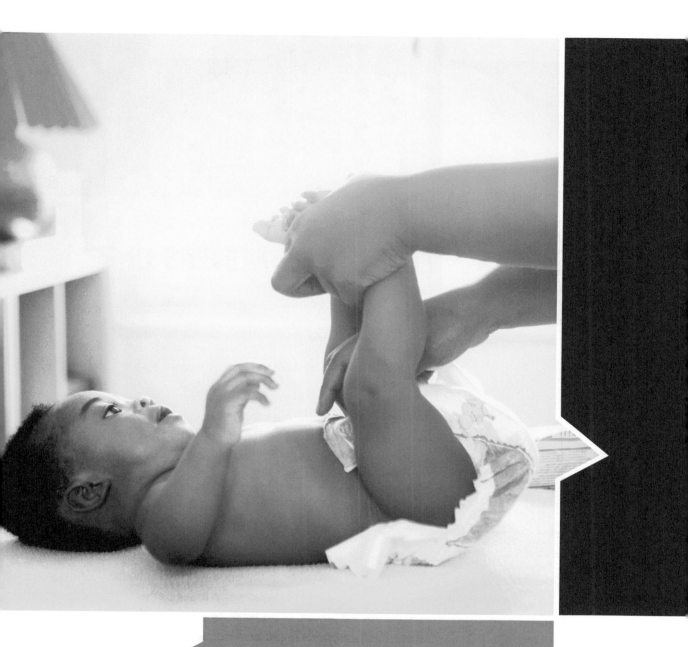

What did your parents do for you that you did not appreciate until you were older?

QUESTION *#1*

#BSFLmindset

We can trust God is at work on our behalf.

THE BIBLE MEETS LIFE

I live in Oklahoma. Tornado Alley. I'm no stranger to storms that drop down out of nowhere and cause total devastation. I've seen entire communities leveled and I've helped families sift through the rubble searching for any remnant of their homes. It's heart-wrenching.

No one is immune from crisis. We may not have lost a home or encountered a tornado, but we've all felt the devastating winds of hard times. We've all found ourselves rocked by a storm of life and left picking up the pieces.

Here's one thing we can be sure of: even though we may be caught off guard or surprised by a crisis, God certainly is not. In fact, He's never surprised by any problem we have.

As we conclude our look at the life of Joseph, we can see how God prepared and led him in both the good times and the hard times. God is always working, and He has a plan to see us though any crisis. While our problems may seem huge, God is bigger than anything that may happen to us. We can trust His plan to help us overcome.

WHAT DOES THE BIBLE SAY?

Genesis 50:15-21 *(HCSB)*

15 When Joseph's brothers saw that their father was dead, they said to one another, "If Joseph is holding a grudge against us, he will certainly repay us for all the suffering we caused him."

16 So they sent this message to Joseph, "Before he died your father gave a command:

17 'Say this to Joseph: Please forgive your brothers' transgression and their sin—the suffering they caused you.' Therefore, please forgive the transgression of the servants of the God of your father." Joseph wept when their message came to him.

18 Then his brothers also came to him, bowed down before him, and said, "We are your slaves!"

19 But Joseph said to them, "Don't be afraid. Am I in the place of God?

20 You planned evil against me; God planned it for good to bring about the present result—the survival of many people. **21** Therefore don't be afraid. I will take care of you and your little ones." And he comforted them and spoke kindly to them.

Key Words

Transgression (v. 17)— This translation of one of three main Hebrew words for sin denotes a defiant violation of God's law, a brazen revolt, rebellion.

Genesis 50:15-17

For 17 years, Jacob lived in Egypt with all his sons and their families (see Gen. 47:28). He'd formerly considered his life hard and difficult (v. 9), but his closing years were spent in security with his sons. After Jacob died, his 12 sons took his body back home and buried him with his wife and ancestors.

They could not bury the past, however. The brothers once again felt shame and fear because of how they treated Joseph in their youth. After the loss of their father, they became afraid that Joseph would finally seek his revenge.

For his part, Joseph had cared for his family for 17 years, continually ensuring their safety and provision. Every indication is that the family—and everyone in it—greatly prospered under Joseph's watchful care. Even so, the whirlwind of fear and the storm of disgrace threatened the fabric of healing that had covered them for so many years.

> **When have you found forgiveness hard to accept or believe?**
>
> QUESTION **#2**

Afraid at first to come in person, the brothers sent a somewhat deceitful message to Joseph to again seek his forgiveness for their terrible sin. This was potentially dangerous, given their history. The Bible tells us that Satan roams about like a roaring lion seeking those he can devour (see 1 Pet. 5:8). He looks for any crack—any way he can enter, steal our peace, and cause alarm. The brothers had lost their peace.

To be fair, they could have chosen to plot against Joseph again, but they didn't. Apparently, they finally learned their lesson. Instead, they sought forgiveness—again—for what they had done. And as they did, they acknowledged their actions as sin.

Joseph was tremendously affected by the confession of his brothers. After all these years, they still had such fear of him and thought he had not truly forgiven them. Joseph discovered that reassurance was still needed.

Past issues often have a way of coming back around again—especially if we haven't completely dealt with them. The key to surviving a return attack of the enemy is to deal with it head on. Take determined action not to allow past hurts and issues to regain traction or grow within you again.

WHAT IS TRUST?

Which of the above images best illustrates your understanding of what it means to trust God? Explain.

Which image best illustrates your understanding of what it means to trust other people? Explain.

> *What can it cost us to leave justice in God's hands?*

QUESTION **#3**

Genesis 50:18-19

Joseph had once dreamed that his brothers would bow before him (see Gen. 37:5-9). That dream was fulfilled when his brothers first stood before him seeking grain (see Gen. 42:9). At that time, they bowed before him out of respect for his office; but now years later, they bowed before him in fear. They entered Joseph's presence and offered themselves as his slaves.

In other words, they recognized that they belonged to Joseph. They'd been captured by their own actions and lies years earlier, and holding onto our fears always makes us slaves to those fears.

Joseph also could have allowed himself to become enslaved, as well. His brothers were enslaved to fear, and he could have joined them by being enslaved to bitterness or a desire for payback. But Joseph refused to be shackled again.

Instead, Joseph humbled himself before God, recognizing that it was not his place to punish his brothers. He refused to turn his back on what God had shown him so many years before—that God was in control and had brought him to Egypt to save his family.

To trust is to commit one's care or keeping to another. The life of Joseph demonstrates over and over again that God can be trusted. We can commit our care and keeping to Him. In legal terms, a trust is a relationship between parties in which one person (the trustee) has the power to manage, and the other person (the beneficiary) has the privilege of receiving the benefits.

Joseph decided early in his life to make God his Trustee and to live as His beneficiary. By allowing God to control the consequences of his brothers' actions, Joseph freed himself from the constraint of revenge. **It was better to trust God to be God and let Him do what needed to be done.**

Genesis 50:20-21

Notice that Joseph didn't dismiss what his brothers had done all those years ago. He described their plan as evil. But he also recognized that God had His own plan. God worked in spite of the brothers' hatred, transforming the mistreatment of Joseph into deliverance for a nation, rescue for a family, and salvation for all people.

Indeed, God intended good to come from their actions—the salvation of many people.

Joseph could now see the big picture. God had worked for good in his life, and Joseph intended to do the same. "Therefore don't be afraid. I will take care of you and your little ones." Joseph didn't roll his eyes at his brothers' long-standing fear. Instead, "he comforted them and spoke kindly to them." His words and actions spoke reassurance. Joseph brought them strength and encouragement.

When I read the story of Joseph, I'm reminded of Jesus—the beloved Son of our Heavenly Father. Jesus stood before the nation of Israel and offered them life. When the religious leaders saw the love the people had for Jesus, they became jealous and conceived a plan to murder Him. But God had a different plan. He took the hate of the people and used it to extend grace to a lost and dying world.

As Jesus' earthly ministry was nearing its end, He sat down for a meal with His disciples. At that last meal, He laid the future out for them. He told them, "Your heart must not be troubled or fearful" (John 14:27). Jesus also called them to "Be courageous " (John 16:33). Jesus knew the big picture and desired for His followers—including us—to trust Him.

> *For us, what are the implications of the statement "Don't be afraid"?*
>
> QUESTION **#4**

> *How can we encourage one another to consider our lives from God's perspective?*
>
> QUESTION **#5**

LIVE IT OUT

What does it look like to actively trust God in your everyday life? Consider the following suggestions:

▶ **Trust Jesus.** Submit your life to Jesus and receive forgiveness for your sins.

▶ **Be courageous.** Identify an area of life in which fear has held you back. Ask God to help you let go of that fear and move forward with confidence according to His plan.

▶ **Spread the word.** Record the story of a time you benefited from trusting God. Share that story with someone else.

God is real, and He is really in control during the hard times of our lives—and in the good times, as well. Even when we can't see the big picture, He can see it. He knows the storms we will face, and He is worthy of our trust.

Meeting God at the Intersection of Expectation and Disappointment

A little more than a month after his son's tragic death by suicide, Pastor Rick Warren made what some might consider to be a disturbing admission. He confessed that he had prayed regularly and sincerely for a different outcome to his son's life. "For 27 years I prayed every day of my life for God to heal my son's mental illness," Warren declared. "It was the number one prayer of my life."

To continue reading "Meeting God at the Intersection of Expectation and Disappointment" from *Mature Living* magazine, visit biblestudiesforlife.com/articles.

My group's prayer requests

....
....
....
....
....
....
....
....
....
....
....
....

My thoughts

Overcome: Living Beyond Your Circumstances

For the past six sessions, we have walked alongside Joseph and learned some key principles to help us rise above and overcome even the most challenging circumstances.

Christt

We are ultimately overcomers because Jesus Christ overcame sin and death for us. Christ empowers us with His Holy Spirit so that we can stand strong. In Christ, we have a citizenship in heaven, which moves us beyond seeing things just from the world's vantage point. We can forgive others because we have experienced forgiveness from Christ.

Community

When hard times hit, the church and family support each other and stand together. God's design is that we never go through difficult circumstances alone. The church is to be the one place where our purpose and service are valued.

Culture

The world knows nothing more than what this earth has to offer. From the world's viewpoint, you don't live beyond your circumstances; you merely endure them. Believers can model purpose and joy in spite of circumstances, and in so doing, they can show the world that life in Christ takes us beyond an earthly mindset.

GENERAL INSTRUCTIONS

In order to make the most of this study and to ensure a richer group experience, it's recommended that all group participants read through the teaching and discussion content in full before each group meeting. As a leader, it is also a good idea for you to be familiar with this content and prepared to summarize it for your group members as you move through the material each week.

Each session of the Bible study is made up of three sections:

1. THE BIBLE MEETS LIFE.

An introduction to the theme of the session and its connection to everyday life, along with a brief overview of the primary Scripture text. This section also includes an icebreaker question or activity.

2. WHAT DOES THE BIBLE SAY?

This comprises the bulk of each session and includes the primary Scripture text along with explanations for key words and ideas within that text. This section also includes most of the content designed to produce and maintain discussion within the group.

3. LIVE IT OUT.

The final section focuses on application, using bulleted summary statements to answer the question "So what?" As the leader, be prepared to challenge the group to apply what they learned during the discussion by transforming it into action throughout the week.

For group leaders, this leader guide contains several features and tools designed to help you lead participants through the material provided.

QUESTION 1: ICEBREAKER

These opening questions and/or activities are designed to help participants transition into the study and begin engaging the primary themes to be discussed. Be sure everyone has a chance to speak, but maintain a low-pressure environment.

DISCUSSION QUESTIONS

Each "What Does the Bible Say?" section features at least four questions designed to spark discussion and interaction within your group. These questions encourage critical thinking, so be sure to allow a period of silence for participants to process the question and form an answer.

This leader guide also contains follow-up questions and optional activities that may be helpful to your group, if time permits.

DVD CONTENT

Each video features Alex Himaya teaching about the primary themes found in the session. We recommend you show this video in one of three places: (1) at the beginning of group time, (2) after the icebreaker, or (3) after a quick review and/or summary of "What Does the Bible Say?" A video summary is included as well. You may choose to use this summary as background preparation to help you guide the group.

The leader guide contains additional questions to help unpack the video and transition into the discussion. For a digital leader guide with commentary, see the "Leader Tools" folder on the DVD-ROM in your Bible study kit.

Note: For helps on how to use Bible Studies for Life, tips on how to better lead groups, or additional ideas for leading this Bible study, visit www.ministrygrid.com/web/biblestudiesforlife.

SESSION 1: OVERCOME BETRAYAL

The Point: God is at work, even when it's not obvious.

The Passage: Genesis 37:19-27; 39:1-2

The Setting: While Joseph's brothers were tending to their father's flocks, Jacob/Israel sent Joseph to check on them. The brothers spotted Joseph coming toward them and quickly hatched a plan to dispose of him, adjusting the plan as they went. They sold him to traders who in turn sold him to Potiphar, the captain of Pharaoh's guard in Egypt. All the while, God was with Joseph and made him successful serving his Egyptian master.

QUESTION 1: What did sibling rivalry look like at your house?

> *Optional activity:* Draw attention to the point of this session by asking group members to spend two or three minutes thinking of items or forces that are present with you in your meeting place, yet are not visible. Use the example of cellular signals to get the ball rolling.

Video Summary: Alex opens the study by talking about how the Book of Genesis lays out the great design for God's redemption plan—from the beginning, to the fall, to the flood, to the call of Abraham, and the promise that a Redeemer would come. As that promise unfolds, we see how it involves Joseph. Joseph was given a dream he didn't understand. He didn't know he carried a message that would unlock the mercy and love of God in a tangible way. Joseph reveals a picture of long-suffering, redemption, and reconciliation.

WATCH THE DVD SEGMENT FOR SESSION 1. THEN USE THE FOLLOWING QUESTIONS AND DISCUSSION POINTS TO TRANSITION TO THE STUDY.

- Joseph went from the pit to the palace, but not overnight. It took time. It was difficult. What things can we know about Joseph just from observing his journey?

- Joseph felt pain, endured loneliness, and experienced betrayal. Likely there were times he wondered what God was up to or if God was working at all. Sound familiar? What might others know about *you* just from observing your journey?

WHAT DOES THE BIBLE SAY?

ASK FOR A VOLUNTEER TO READ ALOUD GENESIS 37:19-27; 39:1-2.

Response: What's your initial reaction to these verses?

- What do you like about the text?

- What questions do you have about these verses?

TURN THE GROUP'S ATTENTION TO GENESIS 37:19-24.

QUESTION 2: What's your gut reaction to Joseph's betrayal?

The goal here is to ask this question immediately after reading Genesis 37:19-24. Give group members an opportunity to respond verbally to Joseph's betrayal at the hands of his own family, imagining what it would be like for a group of brothers to want to kill their own.

> *Optional follow-up:* What ideas or images come to mind when you hear the word *betrayal*?

QUESTION 3: What are our options when we feel betrayed?

We all have choices when we feel betrayed. This question is intended to help group members think through what their options are when they face betrayal. In answering this question, you may want to encourage members to consider what has and hasn't worked in the past, as well as what they know to be true about who God is.

> **Optional activity:** Encourage group members to complete the activity "Stories of Betrayal" on page 9. If time allows, ask volunteers to share their responses.

MOVE TO GENESIS 37:25-27.

QUESTION 4: Since God is always at work, what's our responsibility when we can't see what He's doing?

This question is intended to help group members see the relationship between the truth that God is always at work—whether we can see it or not—and our responsibility to live out what we believe in the day to day.

> **Optional follow-up:** What steps can we take to identify God's work during difficult situations?

CONTINUE WITH GENESIS 39:1-2.

QUESTION 5: Even after betrayal, how do we behave in ways that show God is at work?

Encourage group members to be specific in their responses to this application question. What are some concrete, practical behaviors that reveal our trust that God is at work?

> **Optional follow-up:** How can we help one another behave in ways that show God is at work?

Note: The following question does not appear in the Bible study book. Use it in your group discussion as time allows.

QUESTION 6: God will never betray or abandon us. How can believing this truth influence our actions and attitudes each day?

Using a biblical truth as foundation, this question will give group members an opportunity to connect how living out the truths of our beliefs can impact our lives and the lives of others as we go about our day. Encourage group member to share specific examples.

LIVE IT OUT

We choose our responses to betrayal. Invite group members to consider these suggestions for trusting God even when they don't know what He's doing.

- **Look back.** Make a list of the different ways God has worked in and through your life in recent years.
- **Forgive yourself.** Identify a failure or shortcoming from the past that still produces guilt in your life. Choose to let go of that failure and trust in God's ability to work for your good.
- **Forgive others.** Identify a betrayal that continues to impact your life. Take a step this week to move toward forgiveness and healing in that relationship.

Challenge: We all experience betrayal. We all experience times when we cry out to God—maybe even times when we wonder if He's really there. Thankfully, we can trust that God is always at work to carry us through those moments, just as He carried Joseph. As you move through this next week, try to be conscious of times when you feel betrayed and watch for how God is working in the midst of those feelings. Set your focus there rather than on how you feel wronged.

Pray: Ask for prayer requests and ask group members to pray for the different requests as intercessors. As the leader, close this time by committing the members of your group to the Lord and asking Him to give each of you strength and courage when you feel betrayed, trusting that He is working on your behalf.

SESSION 2: OVERCOME TEMPTATION

The Point: It's easier to resist temptation when you know what's at stake.

The Passage: Genesis 39:3-12

The Setting: God blessed Joseph and his service so thoroughly that his master placed Joseph over the entire household and all his possessions. Even the master's wife was impressed with Joseph and repeatedly tried to seduce him. In his loyalty to his master and to God, Joseph just as repeatedly turned aside her advances as evil and a "sin against God."

QUESTION 1: What are some warning labels you always ignore?

> *Optional activity:* Choose an item from your meeting space, then ask group members to brainstorm interesting or outrageous warning labels for that item—suggestions can be funny or serious. Repeat with different items as time allows. Encourage group members to have fun with this. **Note:** Consider offering a sample answer to this question, such as "Dry clean only," so that group members know you're asking about practical warning labels, not something overly spiritual.

Video Summary: In this session Alex talks about temptation. There is a power struggle between the flesh and the spirit. The struggle is real and it's present. But we live with the promise that God will right the wrong. Until then, there is a war going on. For Joseph this became very real when he encountered Potiphar's wife. As he walked through this temptation, he probably gave thought to his past—the pit, the slavery—as well as the possibilities for his future. Joseph trusted God and ran from temptation. And God was faithful to him.

WATCH THE DVD SEGMENT FOR SESSION 2. THEN USE THE FOLLOWING QUESTIONS AND DISCUSSION POINTS TO TRANSITION TO THE STUDY.

- When you look at the choices in your life, in what ways do you see temptations as opportunities for obedience to God?

- What do you think it is about looking back and looking forward that helps us resist temptation?

WHAT DOES THE BIBLE SAY?

ASK FOR A VOLUNTEER TO READ ALOUD GENESIS 39:3-12.
Response: What's your initial reaction to these verses?

- What questions do you have about these verses?

- What application do you hope to gain about resisting temptation?

TURN THE GROUP'S ATTENTION TO GENESIS 39:3-6.
QUESTION 2: What characteristics suggest God is with someone?

This question will give group members an opportunity to articulate, based on Genesis 39:3-6, what it means to have God's presence in their lives and what might be some concrete examples of that presence.

Optional follow-up: What are some of the ways you've experienced God's blessing in your life?

Optional activity: Encourage group members to complete the activity "What's At Stake?" on page 19. If time permits, ask for volunteers to share their responses.

MOVE TO GENESIS 39:7-10.

QUESTION 3: What's at stake when we give in to temptation?

Defining what's at risk helps group members understand the importance of putting a plan in place ahead of time to avoid the temptation, rather than trying to repair the damage once it has occurred. As the leader, make sure you guide the discussion in this direction.

QUESTION 4: What's at stake when we resist temptation?

This question applies to the negative consequences we might experience when we choose to resist temptation. For example, by rejecting the illicit offer from Potiphar's wife, Joseph ran the risk of offending someone who had the power to harm him. His freedom was at stake.

Optional follow-up: What do these verses teach us about the nature of sin?

CONTINUE WITH GENESIS 39:11-12.

QUESTION 5: What's the difference between resisting temptation and fleeing from temptation?

The goal of this question is to help group members evaluate different responses to temptation. Sometimes we can stand firm against temptation and continue with our normal lives; other times such resistance won't work and we must flee. How do we know which response is appropriate?

Optional follow-up: As followers of Jesus who still struggle with sin, how can we avoid giving in to temptation?

Note: The following question does not appear in the Bible study book. Use it in your group discussion as time allows.

QUESTION 6: As a group, how can we support one another through temptation in ways that are both practical and appropriate?

This question is included to encourage biblical community among your group members. Belonging to redemptive community is an important aspect of overcoming hardships in life. Focus your discussion on specific ways group members can support one another.

Optional follow-up: It has been said, "It's one thing to want to win. It's another to plan to win." How might this philosophy be applied to temptation? Be specific.

LIVE IT OUT

We all encounter temptation from time to time. Invite group members to consider the following suggestions for making the right choice.

- **Look inside.** The first step in fleeing temptation is recognizing that temptation springs from our own desires (see Jas. 1:14). Spend a few moments evaluating which inner desires often tempt you to do wrong.

- **Remember what's at stake.** When faced with temptation, we always have a choice. Choose to consider the consequences (spiritual, relational, physical, etc.) *before* you choose to sin.
- **Remember God's Word.** Memorize 1 Corinthians 10:13 as a reminder that temptation always creates a choice.

Challenge: Wouldn't life be easier if temptations came with warning labels? Sin promises great things up front, but it's only after we give in that we learn about the consequences. Consider asking a close friend—someone you truly trust—to step into your life and be honest with you when you are headed toward temptation and he or she sees warning signs that you may not. Be willing to do the same for others.

Pray: Ask for prayer requests and ask group members to pray for the requests as intercessors. Encourage them to ask God—silently or out loud—to help them move beyond temptation and make the right choices.

SESSION 3: OVERCOME BEING FORGOTTEN

The Point: Keep doing what God has gifted you to do.

The Passage: Genesis 39:21-23; 40:5-8,20-23

The Setting: In return for his purity and integrity in refusing the advances of his master's wife, Joseph wound up in prison. Even there God blessed him and gave him favor in the warden's eyes. Two of Pharaoh's out-of-favor officials were in prison and had disturbing dreams. Joseph, with God's insight, interpreted the dreams, asking only that one official, about to be restored to Pharaoh's service, remember Joseph when that day came.

QUESTION 1: When have you rediscovered something you forgot you had?

Optional activity: Have fun with the theme of forgetfulness by playing a memory game with your group. Start by saying a single word of your choice. Then, the person on your right must repeat your word and add a new word. Continue around the circle, adding a new memory word for each participant. The game ends (or starts again) when someone fails to correctly repeat the entire string of words.

Video Summary: In this session Alex talks about how God has gifted us, referencing 1 Corinthians 12 as well as Exodus 31, where men were gifted for the purpose of creating the many details of the tabernacle. God, through His Spirit, gives gifts, and the purpose of these gifts is to put all the attention on the Almighty God—from ornaments of the tabernacle, to priestly garments, to teaching the Word of God with boldness. All gifts exist to point people to God. And just as Joseph took his circumstances and his gifting and put them to work, we are called to serve, using our gifts and talents, in whatever arena we find ourselves.

WATCH THE DVD SEGMENT FOR SESSION 3. THEN USE THE FOLLOWING QUESTIONS AND DISCUSSION POINTS TO TRANSITION TO THE STUDY.
- What are the gifts and talents you have? What are the things you love doing?
- Whether it's your pit, your palace, or anything in between, how are you using your gifting to influence the kingdom of God?

WHAT DOES THE BIBLE SAY?

ASK FOR A VOLUNTEER TO READ ALOUD GENESIS 39:21-23; 40:5-8,20-23.

Response: What's your initial reaction to these verses?

- What questions do you have about these verses?
- What new application do you hope to get from this passage?

TURN THE GROUP'S ATTENTION TO GENESIS 39:21-23.

QUESTION 2: How do we remain faithful when we find ourselves where we didn't expect to be?

This application questions will draw on feelings and emotions that come from a familiar experience we all face at one time or another—finding ourselves where we didn't expect to be. Joseph's life serves as a good example. Consider asking group members to identify specific ways that Joseph remained faithful as they respond.

Optional follow-up: What are some of the ways God has gifted us to carry out His work?

MOVE TO GENESIS 40:5-8.

QUESTION 3: What are some little things that allow us to demonstrate God's concern to others?

This question is intended to help group members see that every action taken to help others doesn't have to be a grand gesture. Sometimes little steps produce big results. Encourage group members to think of their own contexts—at home, at work, and in the community—when brainstorming little things that demonstrate God's care and concern.

Optional follow-up: When have you been blessed because of the care and concern of others?

CONTINUE WITH GENESIS 40:20-23.

QUESTION 4: When have you felt forgotten?

This question gives group members an opportunity to share a story. Sharing and storytelling represent great ways for growing as a group. This question creates an environment for sharing relative to the text. If group members seem hesitant to share, consider stepping out and sharing a story of your own first.

Optional follow-up: How do you typically react when others forget you or fail to acknowledge you?

QUESTION 5: How do we support one another to keep doing what God has gifted us to do?

Begin your discussion by challenging group members to think beyond their own lives to how they can help one another continue to do what it is God has gifted them to do. This question will help your group build community and accountability by identifying specific actions they can take to encourage one another.

Optional activity: Direct group members to complete the activity "Your Gift" on page 31. If time allows, encourage volunteers to share their ideas for how they can use their gifting in their church, family, community, and work—things they haven't pursued before.

Note: The following question does not appear in the Bible study book. Use it in your group discussion as time allows.

QUESTION 6: What are some everyday obstacles that hinder us from using our gifts to benefit God's kingdom?

By identifying specific obstacles they have encountered in using their gifts, group members will have an opportunity to examine why those things have been obstacles and how best to avoid them moving forward.

LIVE IT OUT

Encourage group members to consider these options for remaining engaged even when they feel forgotten.

- **Discover your gifts.** Use a spiritual-gifts assessment to identify the ways God has equipped you to serve.

- **Sharpen your skills.** Use a tool like the Ministry Grid (MinistryGrid.com) to gain training for different areas of ministry that connect with your natural gifts.

- **Make a difference.** Jump in with both feet to serve God and others. Find an area of need in your church or community, and use your gifts to serve with excellence.

Challenge: Joseph went from being the favored son to slave to prisoner. But even in prison he managed to distinguish himself with excellence. An Egyptian prison surely was a far cry from where Joseph expected to be, but instead of wallowing in self-pity, he continued to serve. Revisit Genesis 39:21-23 this week. When things don't go as you expect, keep Joseph in mind and focus on how you can do what God has gifted you to do anyway.

Pray: Ask for prayer requests and ask members to pray for the different requests as intercessors. As the leader, close this time by asking the Lord for His presence with each of you when you feel forgotten. Ask the Lord for strength and courage not to be defeated by your circumstances but instead to trust Him and what He has gifted you to do.

SESSION 4: OVERCOME HARD TIMES

The Point: God has a plan to see you through any crisis.

The Passage: Genesis 41:28-36,46-49

The Setting: When Pharaoh had a perplexing dream, his restored official suddenly remembered Joseph's dream interpretation and commended him to Pharaoh. After being fetched from prison, Joseph, again with insight from God, interpreted the dream: God was warning Pharaoh of things to come—seven years of abundance followed by seven years of famine. Joseph even laid out a strategy for leveraging the abundant years for survival during the barren years. Pharaoh appointed Joseph to implement the strategy, which he did.

QUESTION 1: What is your number one survival tip to prepare for a crisis?

Optional activity: Supplement the idea of God's plan by displaying a set of blueprints for your group to examine. This can be an actual set of blueprints or a printed sample from online. It doesn't matter what kind of building it is connected with—the idea is simply to display the complicated design that goes into constructing any physical structure in the modern world. Encourage group members to share their reactions after observing the blueprints for a few moments. **Note:** Display the blueprints in whatever way is most appropriate for your group. Hang them on the wall, spread them out on the floor, distribute individual samples for each person, and so on.

Video Summary: In this session Alex talks about crisis. The Bible holds many real stories of crisis: Cain and Abel; the flood; Noah and his sons; Jacob and Esau; and Joseph and his brothers. Why all these accounts of strife? What is God revealing about Himself? In the midst of trials and hard times, God is still very much in control. Often our problems point us, guide us, and direct us right where God wants us to go. Joseph couldn't just go from a coat of many colors to the throne of Pharaoh. God had created a road map and Joseph was on it.

WATCH THE DVD SEGMENT FOR SESSION 4. THEN USE THE FOLLOWING QUESTIONS AND DISCUSSION POINTS TO TRANSITION TO THE STUDY.

- How can Joseph's story help you make the choice to rest in the perfect purposes of God rather than get stuck in the crisis?

- Think about the road you are on. In what ways can you see how God has been molding and shaping you to bring you to this point?

WHAT DOES THE BIBLE SAY?

ASK FOR A VOLUNTEER TO READ ALOUD GENESIS 41:28-36,46-49.
Response: What's your initial reaction to these verses?

- What do you like about the text?

- What new application do you hope to receive about God's plan to see you through hard times?

TURN THE GROUP'S ATTENTION TO GENESIS 41:28-32.
QUESTION 2: What does God's warning tell us about His character?

This observation question will allow group members greater insight into the character of God through a closer examination of Genesis 41:28-32. Filter all discussion through the lens of this passage.

Optional follow-up: What are some ways God prepared Joseph for his audience with Pharaoh?

MOVE TO GENESIS 41:33-36.
QUESTION 3: When has God given you a clear picture of what to do?

It may be best for you as the leader to answer this question first. If group members seem hesitant to respond— or seem hesitant to reveal something that feels like bragging—offer your own story as an example.

Optional follow-up: What are some ways we can actively search for God's plan in connection with our lives?

CONTINUE WITH GENESIS 41:46-49.
QUESTION 4: When we don't have a clear picture from God, how can we actively pursue His solution?

Use Joseph's life, experiences, and actions as a foundation for your discussion. Some group members will be able to contribute to the discussion based on past experience. Encourage others to share based on a plan that will prepare them for the time when they encounter this kind of situation themselves.

Optional activity: Direct group members to complete the activity "Your Plan" on page 41. If time allows, encourage volunteers to share some of their goals.

QUESTION 5: How is God preparing our group for present and future challenges?

Focus your discussion on ways group members see God working to prepare your group for challenges. Responses may indicate how God is preparing you as individuals to come together to face challenges. Others may relate to how God is knitting you together as a group and in so doing is preparing you to move forward as a community.

Optional follow-up: How is God preparing you personally for present and future challenges?

Note: The following question does not appear in the Bible study book. Use it in your group discussion as time allows.

QUESTION 6: What decisions must we make in order to benefit from God's plans for our lives?

Ending group time with this application question should leave group members with a sense of action. Encourage them to be specific in their responses.

LIVE IT OUT

Since we're best served by following God's plan during a crisis, what should we do in the meantime? Invite group members to consider the following ideas.

- **Look behind.** Make a list of the ways God has prepared you for where you are today. Be specific.
- **Look up.** Set aside time this week to thank God for His provision in your life. Praise Him as the Source of your successes and of your ability to handle trials.
- **Look around.** Make yourself available to others. Ask the Lord to lead you to someone this week who is in difficulty or crisis, and use your gifts to help in a practical way.

Challenge: We will all go through hard times. We'll have to make decisions in the middle of a crisis. And in that moment, we'll do well to remember that God already has a plan to see us through. Reflect this week on times God has seen you through a crisis in the past. Thank Him for His care. Allow yourself to rest in the assurance that He has been faithful before, and He will be faithful again.

Pray: Ask for prayer requests and ask group members to pray for the requests as intercessors. As the leader, close this time by acknowledging that God is bigger than any crisis you will face. Thank Him in advance for preparing and guiding each of you through hard times. Ask for His help to overcome in the midst of your struggles.

SESSION 5: OVERCOME BITTERNESS

The Point: Relationships can only move forward with forgiveness.

The Passage: Genesis 45:3-11

The Setting: The famine was widespread. Joseph's father heard Egypt had food and sent his sons to purchase some. Joseph recognized his brothers when they came, though they did not recognize him. After a series of tests, Joseph eventually revealed his identity to them, stressed God had placed him there to keep them alive, and urged them to move the whole clan to Egypt so he could better provide for them during the remainder of the famine.

QUESTION 1: How would you describe the taste of bitterness?

Optional activity: Supplement question 1 by providing one or more food items that will allow group members to actually taste something bitter. Options for such foods include grapefruit, ground coffee, ground cinnamon, cocoa, seltzer water, and so on.

Video Summary: Alex's message in this session is about forgiveness as it played out in the life of Joseph. For Joseph, forgiveness was a lesson he kept learning. Joseph still remembered all he had experienced as a younger man. We know what that is like—when we have been betrayed and rejected, we move forward but don't forget. God worked so faithfully in Joseph's life—teaching him, preparing him, and blessing him. Now the moment had come. Joseph had a choice to make. Joseph would forgive and he would give all the credit to God. Joseph's forgiveness brought the family back together after the death of Jacob. Our God is a God of reconciliation.

WATCH THE DVD SEGMENT FOR SESSION 5. THEN USE THE FOLLOWING QUESTIONS AND DISCUSSION POINTS TO TRANSITION TO THE STUDY.

- In what ways has the Lord taught you the true value of reconciliation and forgiveness?
- When Joseph stood before his begging brothers, he had a choice. He could bless or he could curse. He could walk away or he could forgive. Maybe you need to forgive yourself or someone else. What is the next step God wants you to take?

WHAT DOES THE BIBLE SAY?

ASK FOR A VOLUNTEER TO READ ALOUD GENESIS 45:3-11.

Response: What's your initial reaction to these verses?

- What questions do you have about these verses?
- What new application do you hope to get from this passage?

TURN THE GROUP'S ATTENTION TO GENESIS 45:3-4.

QUESTION 2: How can we let go of the past without forgetting it?

This question calls for group members to navigate the tension present in needing to let go of the past but not being able to forget it. Your discussion will likely raise more questions than answers for some. Be willing to leave them to wrestle with this concept on their own. Encourage them to seek God for the answers.

Optional follow-up: What can we learn about Joseph from these verses?

MOVE TO GENESIS 45:5-8.

QUESTION 3: When have you been willing to forgive?

Help participants understand that you're not asking them to share specific details or overly personal information when answering this question. Rather, you'd like them to focus on their own emotions and experiences during a time when they were willing to forgive someone.

Optional follow-up: What do you find most difficult about choosing to forgive those who've wronged you? Why?

CONTINUE WITH GENESIS 45:9-11.

QUESTION 4: How did Joseph's actions in this story mirror God's actions toward us?

Examine Genesis 45:9-11 closely as a group to engage this question in the most effective way, stopping along the way to identify Joseph's specific actions so that group members can more thoroughly draw parallels between Joseph's actions toward his family and God's actions toward us.

Optional follow-up: What one thing from Joseph's story would you most like to share with someone who is experiencing tough times? Why?

QUESTION 5: What actions on our part begin and maintain the process of reconciliation?

The goal of this question is to help group members think through specific actions they must take in order to seek reconciliation.

Optional activity: Direct group members to complete the activity "Listen Up" on page 51. If time allows, encourage volunteers to share their responses.

Note: The following question does not appear in the Bible study book. Use it in your group discussion as time allows.

QUESTION 6: What are some consequences of refusing to seek reconciliation in our relationships?

Seeking reconciliation in our relationships is a choice. This application question is intended to make group members more aware of the consequences and better able to weigh the cost when they choose not to seek reconciliation.

LIVE IT OUT

How can we incorporate forgiveness into our everyday lives? Encourage group members to consider the following steps.

- **Connect with family.** Take time this week to intentionally connect with a family member. Invest in your relationships as a preventative measure against bitterness and strife.

- **Identify your hurts.** Think through the major pain points that cause you to harbor unforgiveness against others. Ask God to help you understand those hurts, but also to forgive even as He has forgiven you.

- **Apologize when necessary.** If you've wronged someone, acknowledge it. Be bold in asking for forgiveness.

Challenge: Are you having trouble forgiving and moving on? Consider spending some time this week making a list of times others have forgiven you. What about times God has forgiven you? Ask Him to help you recall those significant moments. Use these memories as motivation to help you begin the process of forgiving those who may still be keeping you in bondage.

Pray: Ask for prayer requests and ask group members to pray for the requests as intercessors. As the leader, close this time by acknowledging that forgiveness can be difficult when the memory of a hurt continues to pull us back into bitterness. Ask God to help each of you move beyond anything that may be holding you to the past.

SESSION 6: OVERCOME AN EARTHLY MINDSET

The Point: We can trust God is at work on our behalf.

The Passage: Genesis 50:15-21

The Setting: Life in Egypt went smoothly for the clan of Jacob/Israel until he died. At that point, the brothers who had betrayed Joseph so many years before feared for their safety. What if Joseph secretly held a grudge against them but had hidden it for their father's sake? Now that Dad was dead, would Joseph exact revenge? Joseph understood God had been at work in what they had done; He had planned it and produced good from it.

QUESTION 1: What did your parents do for you that you did not appreciate until you were older?

> ***Optional activity:*** Prior to the group meeting, print out a time sheet for each group member, plus a few extras for visitors. Distribute these sheets at the beginning of the session as a way to reinforce the truth that God is always at work on our behalf—He never "clocks out" or takes a break. Encourage group members to use their time sheet as a constant reminder that God is working for their good. **Note:** You can easily find printable templates of time sheets by typing "time sheet" into a standard search engine.

Video Summary: We've spent six sessions on one epic journey—the journey of a man named Joseph. Joseph is a product of the grace and mercy of God. Joseph was a vehicle God used to move all of us, Joseph included, one step closer to the cross of Christ. Joseph models for us, in a tangible way, the life of a servant, the life of forgiveness, the benefits of abstaining from sin for a greater prize. Joseph waited patiently for God's promise to be fulfilled. It wasn't easy. It was, in fact, very hard and very heart wrenching. But it was worth it.

WATCH THE DVD SEGMENT FOR SESSION 6. THEN USE THE FOLLOWING QUESTIONS AND DISCUSSION POINTS TO TRANSITION TO THE STUDY.

- God was constantly moving in Joseph's life, refining him, shaping him, revealing to him new things about Himself. How do you see God working in your life, on your behalf?

- In what ways does drawing closer to Christ move you closer to your full potential?

WHAT DOES THE BIBLE SAY?

ASK FOR A VOLUNTEER TO READ ALOUD GENESIS 50:15-21.

Response: What's your initial reaction to these verses?

- What questions do you have about trusting that God is always working on your behalf?

- What new application do you hope to get from this passage?

TURN THE GROUP'S ATTENTION TO GENESIS 50:15-17.

QUESTION 2: When have you found forgiveness hard to accept or believe?

This question provides group members with an opportunity to share a story based on their own experience. Encourage them to be as transparent as they are comfortable being. Be ready with an example of your own.

> ***Optional follow-up:*** What emotions do you typically experience when others ask for your forgiveness?

> ***Optional activity:*** Direct participants to complete the activity "What Is Trust?" on page 59. If time allows, encourage volunteers to share their responses.

MOVE TO GENESIS 50:18-19.

QUESTION 3: What can it cost us to leave justice in God's hands?

Encourage participants to think about this question from several different angles. What can it cost us emotionally, financially, intellectually, relationally, socially, personally, and so on?

> ***Optional follow-up:*** What are some negative consequences of grasping for justice and vengeance with our own hands?

CONTINUE WITH GENESIS 50:20-21.

QUESTION 4: For us, what are the implications of the statement "Don't be afraid"?

This question is designed to give group members an opportunity to go a little deeper with their application of "Don't be afraid" based on their interpretation, or understanding, of Genesis 50:20-21.

Optional follow-up: What factors often cause us to feel afraid in spite of our relationship with God?

QUESTION 5: How can we encourage one another to consider our lives from God's perspective?

This is an application question included as a call to action for your group. It promotes accountability and the need to act based on a biblical mindset.

Note: The following question does not appear in the Bible study book. Use it in your group discussion as time allows.

QUESTION 6: What are some practical steps we can take to increase or intensify our trust in God?

Treat this discussion as an opportunity to help your group members drill one layer deeper and more personally than you did in question 5. Encourage them to identify specific steps they can take individually based on their understanding of this week's study.

Optional follow-up: When in your recent past have you tried to run ahead and take control of a situation because you weren't able see that God was working on your behalf? How can the practical steps you listed in question 6 help you react differently moving forward?

LIVE IT OUT

Invite group members to consider the following suggestions for what it looks like to actively trust God in their everyday lives.

- **Trust Jesus.** Submit your life to Jesus and receive forgiveness for your sins.
- **Be courageous.** Identify an area of life in which fear has held you back. Ask God to help you let go of that fear and move forward with confidence according to His plan.
- **Spread the word.** Record the story of a time you benefitted from trusting God. Share that story with someone else.

Challenge: God is always working, and He has a plan to see us though any crisis. God is bigger than anything that may happen to us. We can trust His plan to help us overcome. Moving forward, work to put into practice what you have learned through this study about the life of Joseph. Spend some time asking the Lord to make you immediately aware of times when you try to take control and to help you trust in Him and His plan instead.

Pray: As the leader, close this final session of *Overcome* in prayer. Ask the Lord to help each of you as you move forward to be reminded daily that God promises to work through our circumstances and equip us to rise above them. Thank Him for giving you the story of Joseph as an example of someone who overcame and lived beyond the circumstances of his life.

Note: If you haven't discussed it earlier, decide as a group whether or not you plan to continue to meet together and, if so, what Bible study options you would like to pursue. Visit lifeway.com/smallgroups for help, or if you would like more studies like this one, visit biblestudiesforlife.com/smallgroups.

ALSO AVAILABLE ...

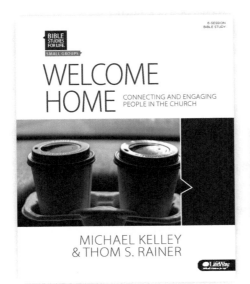
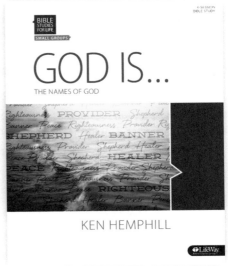
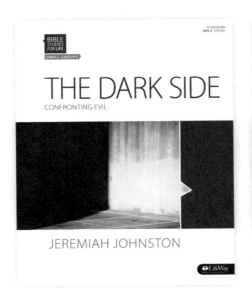